The Largest Stadiums

Susan K. Mitchell
AR B.L.: 6.3
Points: 1.0   M J

MEGASTRUCTURES

THE LARGEST STADIUMS

by Susan K. Mitchell

Gareth Stevens
Publishing

Please visit our web site at: **www.garethstevens.com**
For a free color catalog describing Gareth Stevens Publishing's
list of high-quality books, call 1-800-542-2595 (USA)
or 1-800-387-3178 (Canada).

Library of Congress Cataloging-in-Publication Data

Mitchell, Susan K.
    The largest stadiums / by Susan K. Mitchell.
        p. cm. — (Megastructures)
    Includes bibliographical references and index.
    ISBN-10: 0-8368-8363-2 (lib. bdg.)
    ISBN-13: 978-0-8368-8363-3 (lib. bdg.)
    1. Stadiums. I. Title.
    NA6860.M58   2007
    725'.8043—dc22   2007013147

This edition first published in 2008 by
Gareth Stevens Publishing
A Weekly Reader® Company
1 Reader's Digest Road
Pleasantville, NY 10570-7000 USA

Copyright © 2008 by Gareth Stevens, Inc.

Editorial direction: Mark J. Sachner
Editor: Barbara Kiely Miller
Art direction and design: Tammy West
Picture research: Diane Laska-Swanke
Production: Jessica Yanke
Illustrations: Spectrum Creative Inc.

Picture credits: Cover, title © Philip Gould/CORBIS; p. 5 © DreamWorks/
courtesy Everett Collection; pp. 6, 19, 26 © AP Images; p. 10 © Frederic J.
Brown/AFP/Getty Images; pp. 12, 29 © Panoramic Images/Getty Images;
p. 14 © Doug Pensinger/Getty Images; p. 16 © David Bergman/CORBIS;
p. 17 © James L. Amos/CORBIS; pp. 20-21 © Robert Laberge/Getty Images;
p. 24 © Henry Diltz/CORBIS; p. 27 © Mario Tama/Getty Images

Printed in the United States of America

1 2 3 4 5 6 7 8 9 11 10 09 08 07

CONTENTS

On the Cover: The famous Louisiana Superdome, home of the New Orleans Saints football team, gleams against a backdrop of glittering lights at dusk.

CHAPTER 1

STADIUMS WITH GAME

Touchdown! Goal! Score! Crowds of people pack a stadium to cheer for their favorite sports team. Many different sporting events can be held in a stadium. Football, soccer, baseball, or other sports played on a field can be held there. Some sports, like basketball, are generally held in arenas, not stadiums. The largest stadiums in the world can hold hundreds of thousands of excited sports fans.

Stadiums have been built since the days of ancient Greece. Many Greek stadiums were built out of carved stone or were carved out of a hillside itself. Greek stadiums were usually not completely round like today's stadiums. They were often shaped like a "U" and open at one end. Greek stadiums were used for races and religious celebrations.

Ancient Stadium Architecture

After the Greeks, it was the ancient Romans who took stadiums to a new level. The Romans built massive stone stadiums. Many of them were several hundred feet high. Some early Roman stadiums were open ended like Greek stadiums. Other Roman stadiums were completely rounded and enclosed. They looked more like the stadiums of today.

In the movie *Gladiator*, actor
Russell Crowe (*right*) battles
a wild tiger in the Colosseum.

The most amazing of the ancient Roman stadiums is the Colosseum. Completed in A.D. 80, the Colosseum is still one of the most impressive structures in the world. The twelve-story-high outer wall has hundreds of arches in its design. More than 50,000 people could watch events inside the Colosseum. Much of this beautiful stadium still stands in Rome, Italy, today.

Many stadiums today are bigger and better than the Colosseum. The sporting events held in them are definitely less

Early Extreme Sports

Gladiator games held in Roman stadiums were a dangerous sport. Romans gathered by the thousands in a stadium to watch gladiators fight. It was a kill-or-be-killed blood sport.

Gladiators wore little armor. They usually had only a shield and helmet — if anything at all. Gladiators were divided into different ranks. A gladiator's rank was shown by the type of helmet he wore. What gladiators lacked in armor, they made up for in weapons. They fought each other to the death with swords and other hand-held weapons. The lowest rank of gladiator was made to fight wild animals. The animals were most often mistreated and starved to make them more dangerous.

Most gladiators were usually criminals or slaves. They were forced to fight. A few men, however, actually chose to become gladiators. Gladiators with winning records were often celebrated. They were a kind of celebrity in ancient Rome.

5

Every year, thousands of tourists visit the ruins of the
Colosseum in Rome, Italy.

bloody. The design of modern stadiums, however, has
not changed much over thousands of years.

The first step in building any stadium is a solid
foundation. The Colosseum used a drained lake for its
foundation. Today, giant machines dig deep into the
earth for a stadium's foundation. Enormous steel piles
are driven like nails into the hard layer of bedrock
beneath the ground. After hundreds of piles are in place,

reinforced concrete is poured around them. Together, the piles and concrete create a solid foundation for the framework of the rest of the stadium.

Unlike the cut stone structures of ancient stadiums, modern stadiums are constructed of steel and concrete. Cranes lift enormous steel beams into place to form the frame of the stadium. Builders then add concrete walls around the steel frame to complete the building.

The main difference between ancient stadiums and those of today is a roof. The tops of Greek and Roman stadiums were completely open. Today, sports stadiums often have some kind of roof. They often have partially covered seating, a retractable roof, or a permanent dome that covers the entire stadium.

No matter what the design or how construction has changed, one thing has remained the same for thousands of years. A stadium is a place where people come together to be entertained. Stadiums can become icons, or symbols, of a city or a sport. While their basic shape may stay the same, stadiums can be some of the most exciting structures ever built.

MEGA FACTS

The first Olympic Games were held in Greece in 776 B.C. The Olympics were made up of only one event. Early Olympians competed against each other in sprint races.

HOUSTON ASTRODOME

Most stadiums and arenas have diagrams to show available seating. This diagram shows the sections of seats and the baseball field in the Houston Astrodome.

CHAPTER 2

OLYMPIC PROPORTIONS

The largest stadium in the world was built for very strange reasons. Located in Pyongyang, North Korea, the Rungnado May Day Stadium can hold 150,000 people. The size of a stadium is determined by its capacity — the number of people it can hold at one time. The Rungnado Stadium holds more people than any other stadium today.

Construction of the enormous stadium was completed in 1989. It took two and a half years to build the giant structure. The Rungnado Stadium was officially opened on May 1 of that year. The date was the birthday of Kim Il-Sung, the country's leader at the time, and earned the stadium the nickname "May Day Stadium."

The eight-story-tall Rungnado Stadium was originally built as an Olympic stadium. Seoul, South Korea, was selected to host the 1988 Summer Olympic Games. Kim Il-Sung rushed the construction of an even larger Olympic complex in North Korea. He hoped that North Korea would be selected to co-host the 1988 Olympics. When that did not happen, North Korea boycotted the Olympics.

The outside of the massive Rungnado Stadium is

FACT FILE

The Rungnado May Day Stadium is built on Rungra Island in the Taedong River.

While visiting North Korea, U.S. Secretary of State Madeline Albright attended the Arirang Festival (*above*) in Rungnado Stadium.

covered by a sixteen-arch roof. It looks like an open parachute. The roof covers the stadium seating, but it is open in the middle. More than 11,000 tons (9,979 tonnes) of steel were used in the construction of the roof.

The inside of the Rungnado is even more amazing than its outer structure. The stadium has more than

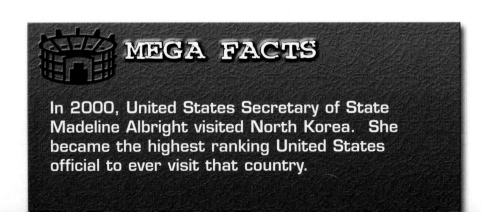

MEGA FACTS

In 2000, United States Secretary of State Madeline Albright visited North Korea. She became the highest ranking United States official to ever visit that country.

2 million square feet (207,000 square meters) of floor space. Its main floor contains a grass soccer field and several rubberized running tracks for foot races.

Several training areas are located on different floors of the Rungnado Stadium complex. Athletes can use an indoor rubberized running track on the sixth floor. They also have access to dining halls, saunas, and sleeping areas. The stadium has nine separate gymnasiums and an indoor swimming pool, too.

All For Show

Few sporting events have been held in the Rungnado May Day Stadium. The stadium is primarily used for celebrating North Korea's rulers. Colorfully costumed and well rehearsed performers participate in mandatory "mass games." In the past, these spectacular shows were held to celebrate former ruler Kim Il-Sung, who died in 1994. Today they are held in honor of his son and

It Takes a Village

Getting selected by the International Olympic Committee to host the Olympics is a tough contest for the world's major cities. Once a city is selected, however, the real work begins. Building a stadium and other structures to host the Olympic Games is a huge task. (In 2007, the U.S. Olympic Committee selected Chicago to represent the United States in its bid to host the 2016 Summer Games.) Stadiums have to be large enough to hold tens of thousands of fans from around the world. They also have to be adaptable enough to host several types of sporting events. Cities also have to construct an "Olympic Village." The village is a group of buildings where the athletes live while competing at the Olympics. Kim Il-Sung not only built an Olympic Stadium without ever having a shot at hosting the Olympics — he also had an Olympic Village built. It included a 3-mile- (5-kilometer-) long stretch of buildings to house athletes.

The Need for Speed

The largest-capacity sports structures in the world are actually racetracks. Some are used for car racing, others for horse racing. Racing facilities are usually called raceways or speedways, not stadiums. They hold more spectators, however, than any stadium in the world.

The largest raceway in the world is the Indianapolis Motor Speedway. It has enough room around the track to seat 250,000 race fans. Built in 1909, it is home to the famous Indy 500 race held each Memorial Day weekend.

the current ruler of North Korea, Kim Jong-II.

The largest mass display held in the Rungnado Stadium is the Arirang Festival. It is a two-month-long festival held each year beginning on April 15. It marks the birthday of Kim Il-Sung. More than 100,000 soldiers, students, and children take part in the performance. In 2005, the normally secretive North Korea allowed outsiders and tourists to attend the Arirang Festival.

The Indianapolis Motor Speedway is the second oldest automotive racetrack in the world. It is nicknamed "The Brickyard" because the track was once completely paved with bricks.

CHAPTER 3

GRIDIRON GIANT

I n the United States, football has become one of the most popular — if not the most popular — of all spectator sports. It makes perfect sense, then, that the biggest stadiums in the United States are football stadiums. What might be surprising, however, is which football stadium is the largest.

The team able to boast of having the largest stadium is not a professional football team. It is the University of Michigan Wolverines. Referred to as The Big House, Michigan Stadium officially holds 107,501 people. It once held, however, an amazing crowd of more than 112,000 football fans.

Thinking Big

The driving force in creating a world class stadium for the University of Michigan was coach Fielding Yost. In the 1920s, he saw the need to expand the football facilities. The team already had a stadium called Ferry Field. Yost

FACT FILE

Melbourne Cricket Grounds is an enormous stadium in Australia that holds more than 100,000 people. The sports of cricket and Australian Rules Football, or "footy," are both played there.

did not want to just expand Ferry Field. He wanted the university to build a completely new stadium.

Convincing the officials at the University of Michigan to put out money for a new stadium was not easy. But Yost held his ground, and by 1926, the university finally approved plans for a new stadium. The university gave the okay for a 72,000-seat stadium with the capacity to be expanded to 100,000 later, if needed.

Building The Big House

The design for Michigan Stadium was a basic bowl stadium design. Yost and his friend, engineer and

Neyland Stadium is the home of the University of Tennesse Volunteers football team. It is the second largest stadium in the United States.

University of Michigan alumnus Bernard Green, had studied stadium design carefully. They agreed that a bowl design would hold the most people and cost the least to build.

Digging the foundation began by fall of 1926. Workers used steam shovels to excavate the site of the new stadium. They even used horses and wagons to help haul away the dirt. After the enormous hole was dug, concrete and steel were used to create the foundation.

Steel beams and wire mesh reinforced the foundation. Workers poured concrete over the steel. In all, 440 tons (400 tonnes) of steel and 31,000 square feet (2,880 sq m) of wire mesh were used. Workers then installed redwood bleachers, laid grass over the football field, and finished painting the stadium. The new Michigan Stadium opened for its first game on October 1, 1927.

Since opening day, The Big House has been through many renovations and expansions.

Home Improvements

In 2006, the officials at the University of Michigan approved plans to renovate Michigan Stadium once again. The overall capacity will not change much. It will reach 108,000 seats at the most. The main changes will be updating the existing facilities.

The plans also call for making the giant stadium more "fan friendly." Additional restrooms will be included and seats will be widened for comfort. More food and beverage stands will be added throughout the stadium. Entrances and exits will also be added to improve safety.

University of Michigan fans rush onto the field after a 2003 win against Ohio State. A record number of people attended the game — 112,118!

In 1949, steel bleachers replaced the wooden ones. The change took the official capacity up to more than 97,000. The stadium's capacity was increased many times in the next 43 years, reaching 102,501. The Big House temporarily lost its title as the largest stadium in the United States in 1996. That year, the University of Tennessee Volunteers expanded Neyland Stadium to hold 102,544 fans.

Not to be outdone, however, the University of Michigan

approved another expansion of Michigan Stadium in 1997. By 1998, 5,000 seats were added, bringing the official capacity of Michigan Stadium to its current 107,501. The Big House was the biggest once again.

Michigan Stadium is the site of many of the university's graduation ceremonies. Some students (*below*) also enjoy being on the field when the stadium is empty.

 MEGA FACTS

It is rumored that one four-leaf clover was planted — to bring the team good luck — when the original grass was laid down in the 1926 Michigan Stadium.

17

CHAPTER 4

SUPER-SIZED FOR SOCCER

Outside the United States, the word "football" means only one thing — soccer. Soccer is the most widely played sport in the world. It is only natural that the most popular sport be played in some of the largest stadiums ever built.

The largest soccer stadium in the world was once the Maracanã in Rio de Janeiro, Brazil. Built in 1950, it was designed to hold an astonishing 200,000 people either seated or standing. At the 1950 World Cup, a record 199,854 soccer fans were in the stadium. Not all of the fans were in seats, however. The stadium had large areas where fans could stand to watch the soccer match.

Constructed of steel and reinforced concrete, the Maracanã is only 78 feet (24 m) high. What makes the Maracanã amazing is its design inside. Two giant rings of seats surround the inside of the almost circular stadium.

Since it was built, the Maracanã has gone through several renovations. Each time, its seating capacity has gone down. Today it holds no more than 100,000 fans. The Maracanã's revisions made way for a new player to emerge in the world's-largest-stadium game.

New Player on the Field

When the Maracanã's capacity shrank, the Estadio Azteca

The Maracanã Stadium (*top left*) has hosted events other than soccer games. In the past, music concerts with as many as **180,000** fans have been held here.

in Mexico City, Mexico, became the world's largest soccer stadium. It can hold more than 105,000 screaming soccer fans at any one time. The Estadio Azteca is built on ground that was once covered by volcanic rock. In 1962, workers began digging the foundation for the stadium. They removed an amazing 200,000 tons

 MEGA FACTS

The official name of the Maracanã Stadium is the Estádio Jornalista Mário Filho. The nickname Maracanã came from the neighborhood where the stadium was built.

The Ultimate Goal

The World Cup is the biggest game in soccer. The championship event began in 1930 and has grown to be one of the greatest sporting events in the world. The World Cup is to the rest of the world what the Super Bowl is to people in the United States. Every four years, the best international professional soccer teams compete in the World Cup finals.

Like the Olympics, hosting the World Cup is a big deal for a country. It comes with prestige, and host countries also make a lot of money. In order for a country to be chosen as host of this tournament, it must have a giant soccer stadium.

(180,000 tonnes) of volcanic rock from the site!

More than 9,000 tons (8,165 tonnes) of steel were used in the foundation and frame of the Estadio Azteca. More than 100,000 tons (90,720 tonnes) of concrete were also used to build the stadium. The giant size of the stadium earned it the nickname "Colossus of Saint Ursula."

In October 2005, the Estadio Azteca was the site of the first National Football League (NFL) regular-season game held outside of the United States. The game was played between the Arizona Cardinals and the San Francisco 49ers.

 MEGA FACTS

Soccer legend Pelé scored his one-thousandth goal at the Maracanã Stadium in 1969.

Playing It Safe

The safety of spectators is very important in the design of any stadium. A stadium must have enough entrances and exits to make sure people can get out in an emergency. Overcrowded stadiums and overly excited fans have led to some of the worst stadium disasters in history.

Throughout the years, people have actually been crushed to death by the push of enormous crowds. Simply leaving a game can be dangerous if there are not enough exits to handle a huge crowd of fans all leaving at the same time. Mexico City's Estadio Azteca has enough exits to completely empty the entire stadium in only eighteen minutes.

A team of eight hundred workers, thirty-four engineers, and ten architects worked together to build the Estadio Azteca. It officially opened on May 29, 1966. Since then, the huge stadium has been home to some incredible events. The Estadio Azteca is the only soccer stadium to host two World Cup events — one in 1970 and another in 1986.

Sporting events are not the only events held in stadiums. Often, they are the sites of huge music concerts or other important world events. Stars like Elton John and groups such as U2 and *NSync have performed before giant crowds at the Estadio Azteca. One of the most important events held at the Estadio Azteca was a visit from Pope John Paul II in 1999.

CHAPTER 5

INCREDIBLE DOME DESIGN

Perhaps the most amazing of all stadiums are the domed stadiums. A dome roof is a structural marvel. A dome roof can cover a huge stadium with very few structural supports. Its rounded shape must, therefore, be incredibly strong. Domed stadiums allow sporting events to be held no matter what the weather is like outside.

The largest fixed domed stadium in the world is the Louisiana Superdome in New Orleans, Louisiana. It can hold more than 72,000 people. A fixed dome is different from other types of domes. The giant domes of some stadiums, like the Georgia Dome in Atlanta, Georgia, are made of a tough fabric that is supported by giant steel cables. The Superdome, however, has a complete, or fixed, domed roof made entirely of steel.

Putting "Super" in the Dome

Workers began digging the foundation for the Louisiana Superdome in 1971. They cleared out 52 acres (21 hectares) of New Orleans swampland for the 13-acre

 FACT FILE

The Pantheon in Rome is one of the oldest known domed structures. It was built completely out of brick and concrete by the ancient Romans.

Eighth Wonder of the World

The Astrodome in Houston, Texas, was the first domed facility of any sport. It was built in 1965 for the Houston Astros baseball team. Originally known as the Colt .45s, the team changed its name when it moved into the new stadium. Summers in Houston are very hot and humid. With a domed ballpark, fans could watch the games in air-conditioned comfort.

Small by stadium standards, the Astrodome only held 50,000 fans at full capacity. The size of the building, however, is an amazing 710 feet (216 m) in diameter. In 2000, the Astrodome was retired as the home of the Houston Astros. Today, the team plays at Minute Maid Park, which has a retractable, or moveable, roof.

Originally built for baseball, the Astrodome was also once the home of the former Houston Oilers football team.

(5-ha) stadium. More than 20,000 tons (18,144 tonnes) of steel were used to build the Superdome. Building the enormous spaceship-shaped stadium took four and one-half years. It opened in November 1975. The New Orleans Saints kicked off the 1975 football season in the Superdome.

At its highest point, the dome is 273 feet (83 m) from ground level. It stretches more than 9 acres (3 ha) across and has a diameter of 680 feet (207 m).

It is an amazing design. The Superdome's strength would be tested, however, in years to come.

Rebuilding the Legend
On August 29, 2005, one of the most deadly hurricanes in U.S. history hit the Gulf Coast. Hurricane Katrina battered New Orleans with a fury. The Superdome

This diagram of Reliant Stadium's retractable roof shows how it can be opened or closed depending on the weather. It takes seven minutes to open or close the roof.

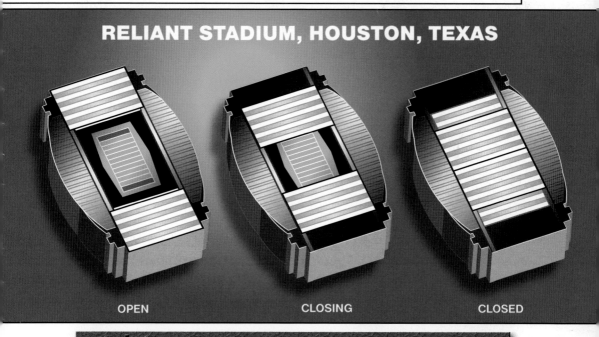

RELIANT STADIUM, HOUSTON, TEXAS

OPEN   CLOSING   CLOSED

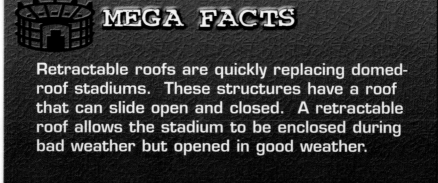

MEGA FACTS

Retractable roofs are quickly replacing domed-roof stadiums. These structures have a roof that can slide open and closed. A retractable roof allows the stadium to be enclosed during bad weather but opened in good weather.

25

Switchback Sports

Most massive stadiums are built for only one sport. A few stadiums, however, can host more than one type of sporting event. They are called multi-use stadiums. Their seats can be moved in and out to create more or less room at ground level. Changing the seating can change the shape and size of a stadium's floor.

Sometimes different ground surfaces can also be added. Some stadium floors are made of artificial playing surfaces. These can be changed depending on the sport being played. A tennis court can become a rubberized gymnasium or track. A hockey rink can become a basketball court.

The **ASPIRE Sports Dome in Doha, Qatar, is the largest domed, indoor multi-purpose sports hall in the world.**

became a shelter for those escaping the winds and rising waters. Though the domed stadium had been used as a shelter during two previous hurricanes, nothing could prepare stadium and city officials for the devastation that would soon follow.

The structure of the Superdome held fast in the raging storm. Despite winds up to 140 miles (225 km) per hour, only two holes were ripped in the steel dome. Each hole was about 20 feet (6 m) long by 5 feet (1.5 m) wide. Nothing could stop the water damage, however, once the levees, or sea walls, broke and New Orleans began flooding on August 30. Water began rushing into the Superdome, but fortunately it climbed no higher than field level.

Eventually, the people sheltered in the Superdome were moved to the Astrodome in Houston and then to other housing. Since the disaster, the Superdome has been rebuilt. Its massive steel dome was repaired and the stadium was improved. The New Orleans Saints reopened the stadium on September 25, 2006, with a game against the Atlanta Falcons. The team and the Superdome survived, the Saints became a sentimental favorite in the NFL playoffs, and fans could once again rock the stadium!

The Louisiana Superdome once again stands proud in the New Orleans skyline now that the damage from Hurricane Katrina has been repaired.

776 B.C. First Olympic Games held in Greece

A.D. 80 Colosseum completed in Rome, Italy

1909 Indianapolis Motor Speedway built; seats 250,000

1927 Michigan Stadium opened; room for 72,000 fans

1950 Maracanã Stadium opened in Rio de Janeiro, Brazil; can hold 200,000 people sitting and standing

1965 Houston Astrodome built; the first domed sports facility

1966 Estadio Azteca opens in Mexico City. With room for 105,000 spectators, it becomes largest stadium after seating in the Maracanã is reduced.

1975 Louisiana Superdome opens; it is the largest fixed-dome stadium in the world with seating for 72,000

1989 Rungnado May Day Stadium opened; seats a record 150,000

1997 Michigan Stadium expands to seat 107,501; becomes largest stadium in the United States

1998 Michigan Stadium holds more than 112,000 fans during a football game, an all-time college record

2000 Secretary of State Madeline Albright becomes the first U.S. official to visit North Korea. She attends a huge celebration at Rungnado Stadium.

2005 Hurricane Katrina hits the Gulf Coast; the Superdome becomes a shelter

2006 The Superdome reopens after repairs

GLOSSARY

adaptable — easily changeable

alumnus – a graduate of a particular school or college

artificial — not natural; man-made

bedrock — a solid rock layer of the earth that lies beneath layers of loose soil

boycotted — refused to attend an event as a form of protest

capacity — the number of people a stadium can safely hold

engineer — someone who uses scientific knowledge to design and build bridges, roads, tunnels, and buildings

excavate — to dig or scoop out an area of ground

fixed domed – describes a solid, immoveable dome structure not supported by steel cables

foundation — the base on which any architectural structure is built

gladiator — a person, often a slave, in ancient Rome who fought in a public arena

icons — important symbols

levees — banks built along bodies of water to keep them from flooding the land

piles — steel beams driven deep into the ground to help support a structure's foundation

prestige — great respect or importance in the opinion of others

professional — in sports, someone who receives money for playing a particular sport

reinforced concrete — concrete with steel bars or mesh added for extra strength and support

retractable — able to be drawn or pulled back

spectators — in sports, people who attend and watch a sporting event

TO FIND OUT MORE

Books

America's Top 10 Construction Wonders. America's Top 10 (series). Tanya Lee Stone (Blackbirch Press)

Football Stadiums. Sports Palaces (series). Thomas S. Owens (Millbrook Press)

Stadiums. Building Amazing Structures (series). Chris Oxlade (Heinemann Library)

Stadiums and Domes. Smart Structures (series). Julie Richards. (Smart Apple Media)

Video

Modern Marvels: Domed Stadiums (A&E Home Video) NR

Web Sites

Estadio Azteca

www.esmas.com/estadioazteca/englishv

Official website of the stadium (English language version)

Michigan Stadium History

bentley.umich.edu/stadium

Stories and photos of The Big House and its history

Stadiums of the World

www.worldstadiums.com

Lists of stadiums of all sizes and their histories

Publisher's note to educators and parents: Our editors have carefully reviewed these Web sites to ensure that they are suitable for children. Many Web sites change frequently, however, and we cannot guarantee that a site's future contents will continue to meet our high standards of quality and educational value. Be advised that children should be closely supervised whenever they access the Internet.

INDEX

About the Author

Susan K. Mitchell lives near Houston, Texas, and loves the stadiums there. As a huge fan of Houston teams, she has been to several of the amazing stadiums in the city — even the famous Astrodome. She is a teacher and author of several children's picture books. Susan has also written many non-fiction chapter books for kids. She has a wonderful husband, two daughters, a dog, and two cats. She dedicates this book to Monica, Doris, and Laura — her biggest cheering section.